AMENDMENTS TO THE UNITED STATES CONSTITUTION
THE BILL OF RIGHTS

DOUBLE JEOPARDY, SELF-INCRIMINATION, AND DUE PROCESS OF LAW

CORONA BREZINA

THE FIFTH AMENDMENT

rosen publishing's
rosen central

New York

Published in 2011 by The Rosen Publishing Group, Inc.
29 East 21st Street, New York, NY 10010

First Edition

Library of Congress Cataloging-in-Publication Data

Brezina, Corona.
The Fifth Amendment: double jeopardy, self-incrimination, and due process of law/Corona Brezina. — 1st ed.
    p. cm. — (Amendments to the United States Constitution: the Bill of Rights)
Includes bibliographical references and index.
ISBN 978-1-4488-1260-8 (library binding)
ISBN 978-1-4488-2306-2 (pbk.)
ISBN 978-1-4488-2313-0 (6-pack)
1. Due process of law—United States—Juvenile literature. [1. United States. Constitution. 5th Amendment—Juvenile literature.] I. Title.
KF4765.B74 2011
345.73'04—dc22

2010018820

Manufactured in the United States of America

CPSIA Compliance Information: Batch #W11YA: For further information, contact Rosen Publishing, New York, New York, at 1-800-237-9932.

On the cover: Background: Former Enron chairman Kenneth Lay took the Fifth Amendment's right against self-incrimination when he testified before a Senate committee in February 2002. Foreground: Tareq and Michaele Salahi refused to answer questions under the Fifth's protection when they were called to testify before the House Homeland Security Committee in January 2010.

CONTENTS

4 INTRODUCTION

8 **CHAPTER ONE**
ROOTS OF THE FIFTH
AMENDMENT

21 **CHAPTER TWO**
THE BILL OF RIGHTS
AND THE FIFTH
AMENDMENT

30 **CHAPTER THREE**
IMPACT OF THE FIFTH
AMENDMENT

43 **CHAPTER FOUR**
THE FIFTH AMENDMENT
TODAY

52 AMENDMENTS
TO THE U.S. CONSTITUTION

55 GLOSSARY

57 FOR MORE INFORMATION

59 FOR FURTHER READING

61 BIBLIOGRAPHY

63 INDEX

INTRODUCTION

The text of the Fifth Amendment of the United States Constitution reads:

No person shall be held to answer for a capital, or otherwise infamous crime, unless on a presentment or indictment of a Grand Jury, except in cases arising in the land or naval forces, or in the Militia, when in actual service in time of War or public danger; nor shall any person be subject for the same offence to be twice put in jeopardy of life or limb; nor shall be compelled in any criminal case to be a witness against himself, nor be deprived of

A police officer reads Miranda rights to a suspect. If the suspect is not Mirandized before police questioning, any statement obtained is inadmissible in court.

life, liberty, or property, without due process of law; nor shall private property be taken for public use, without just compensation.

The U.S. Constitution is the document that established the fundamental structure and operations of the nation's government. Constitutional amendments are measures that have been added to the Constitution in the time since its ratification. The first ten amendments, which make up the Bill of Rights, were added to the Constitution to protect American citizens from potential abuse of government powers.

The Fifth Amendment consists of five provisions that focus on people's rights against government abuse relating to criminal cases. The third clause establishes an individual's right against self-incrimination, which people invoke when "taking the Fifth." This is also the provision in the amendment that grants the right to silence, as conveyed in the Miranda warning that police read to suspects in custody.

The Miranda rights were established in the landmark 1966 case *Miranda v. Arizona*. Ernesto Miranda, who was twenty-three at the time, was arrested for a suspected kidnapping and rape. Evidence pointed to his guilt, and he confessed after two hours of police questioning. Miranda signed a statement confirming that his confession was voluntary. He was convicted and sentenced to twenty years in prison.

But his attorney appealed on the grounds that the confession was not admissible. Miranda had not understood that the Fifth Amendment granted him the right to remain silent. The Sixth Amendment granted him the right to have an attorney present. The Supreme Court agreed, overturning his conviction. The case was a milestone in protecting suspects' constitutional rights.

Because of the constitutional right against self-incrimination, the government cannot force suspects into confession. Prosecutors must instead base their cases on evidence. If there were no protection against self-incrimination, police might be permitted to use coercive, or forceful, techniques—even torture—to obtain confessions.

Every one of the provisions of the Fifth Amendment provides critical protections against potential abuse of power by the government. If Fifth Amendment rights were suspended, federal prosecutors, rather than impartial grand juries, would decide whether or not there was evidence to bring a suspect to trial. When acquitted of an offense in court, defendants could be tried a second time—prosecutors could even prosecute multiple times until receiving a conviction. There would be no just "law of the land" that would require fairness of laws and legal procedures. The government would have the legal right to seize private property without paying the owner.

Although it dates from 1791 and the protections it embodies are much older, the Fifth Amendment is not a historical relic. The amendment continues to guarantee certain valuable protections on a daily basis within the justice system. Interpretation of the Fifth Amendment continues to evolve, too, whenever the Supreme Court hears a case involving a new challenge or proposed expansion of Fifth Amendment rights.

In 2010, the Supreme Court handed down a ruling on *Berghuis v. Thompkins*, a case related to the Miranda warning. The suspect was Mirandized prior to interrogation, but after three hours of questioning, he provided short answers to a few questions. This testimony was eventually used to obtain a conviction. The Supreme Court found that since the suspect was aware of his rights, his response to the questions constituted a waiver of his right to remain silent. Therefore, the evidence was admissible in court. Critics of the ruling claimed that assuming a Miranda waiver could encourage the police to use coercive interrogation techniques to wear down a suspect's resistance. To fully understand the Fifth Amendment, let's begin by taking a look back at its place in history.

CHAPTER ONE

ROOTS OF THE FIFTH AMENDMENT

The framers of the Constitution intended that the Bill of Rights protect ordinary Americans from potential abuses by the government. The Fifth Amendment, in general, safeguards citizens' rights related to criminal cases. Originally, the provisions in the Bill of Rights applied only to federal law. Later, most of these protections were extended to state laws as well, with some exceptions. They do not always apply in civil court, which rules on noncriminal matters.

The Fifth is the longest amendment in the Bill of Rights, consisting of five clauses. Each clause describes a basic constitutional right. Each right has its own background and legal roots. Since the Fifth

Amendment addresses criminal matters, the history behind these rights tends to involve the miscarriage of justice and subsequent efforts to correct these wrongs.

In 1791, when the Bill of Rights was ratified, the framers of the Constitution were forging a new government and envisioning their future as new American citizens. Still, the nation's founders had until recently been British subjects. They had lived their lives under English law. Although Americans had come to resent British rule, the men who drafted the Bill of Rights had great respect for English legal principles. Many elements of English law had become firmly established in the legal systems of the American colonies. When James Madison began drafting the Bill of Rights, many of the possible amendments he considered had roots in English law, including the five clauses of the Fifth Amendment.

Grand Jury

The first clause of the Fifth Amendment establishes a defendant's right to a hearing by a grand jury:

> No person shall be held to answer for a capital, or otherwise infamous crime, unless on a presentment or indictment of a Grand Jury.

Grand jury proceedings are not the same as a court trial. A grand jury convenes in federal cases to determine if to indict, or formally charge, a person with a crime. Instead of ruling on whether the accused individual is guilty or innocent, the grand jury decides if there is compelling evidence to proceed with prosecution of the case. A grand jury generally consists of sixteen to twenty-three citizens, and a majority vote is required to indict. Deliberations and testimony are normally kept secret, and many trial laws do not apply to grand jury proceedings. The prosecutor presents evidence, but neither the accused nor his or her attorney may attend.

The grand jury is the oldest institution incorporated in the Constitution, with its history dating back to the ancient Greek city-state Athens. In the twelfth century, King Henry II of England implemented sweeping legal reforms that included the establishment of a "presenting jury" that would report crimes to royal officials. His new rules and institutions replaced older methods of judgment, such as trial by ordeal, trial by combat, and church courts. The grand jury eventually became one of the pillars of common law, the English legal system based on a history of judges' precedents.

In the seventeenth century, the grand jury began taking on the new role of protecting individuals from unjust prosecution. Since the grand jury consisted of ordinary citizens, the body was independent of influence from the king or the courts. The grand jury could, for example, prevent a government official from prosecuting an individual in court for political reasons. The grand jury became a powerful instrument of justice.

Colonists brought many elements of the common law system, including the grand jury, to

Grand juries convene in federal court—such as the historic Federal Courthouse in Washington, D.C.—to decide whether there is probable cause to indict defendants in federal criminal cases.

America. The earliest reference to the grand jury was in a 1683 charter passed by the elected assembly of New York. As tensions arose between the colonists and the British, the grand jury became an important instrument in protecting American patriots. Grand juries made up of

colonists could refuse to indict individuals targeted for prosecution by British officials.

The Fifth Amendment excludes members of the military from the right to a grand jury hearing:

> . . . except in cases arising in the land or naval forces, or in the Militia, when in actual service in time of War or public danger

Individuals in the armed forces are subject to military trial, not grand jury indictment or trial by jury.

Double Jeopardy

The second clause in the Fifth Amendment protects a defendant from being tried and punished more than once for the same offense:

> . . . nor shall any person be subject for the same offense to be twice put in jeopardy of life or limb

The phrase "jeopardy of life or limb" refers to typical punishments at the time the Constitution was drafted. Criminals could be sentenced to death or mutilation, such as having an ear cut off.

The double jeopardy clause prohibits the courts from trying to convict a defendant for an offense after he or she has already been acquitted, or deemed not guilty, for that offense. It also prohibits a second conviction if the defendant has already been convicted, and it prohibits more than one punishment for a single offense. The double jeopardy prohibition applies to both the federal government and state governments, though not to civil cases. The double jeopardy clause has been frequently contested in court, and judges have imposed limitations on its scope.

United States v. Halper (1989)

In their ruling in a 1989 double jeopardy case, Supreme Court justices quoted directly from the Massachusetts Body of Liberties of 1641, which stated: "No man shall be twise sentenced by Civill Justice for one and the same Crime, offence, or Trespasse." In 1985, Dr. Irving Halper was convicted in criminal court for filing sixty-five false Medicare claims. In the claims, Halper had asked for and received $12 in compensation per claim for medical services for which his company was entitled to only $3, thus defrauding the government out of $585. Halper was sentenced to two years in prison and fined $5,000. The federal government then brought additional civil charges against Halper for filing the claims. These charges would have entitled the government to collect $2,000 for each of the false claims filed (twice the damages) and legal fees. Halper would have had to pay more than $130,000 for his $585 fraud. The district court ruled that the penalty was "entirely unrelated" to the government's damages and would be a second punishment for the crimes. This would violate the double jeopardy clause of the Fifth Amendment. The government appealed directly to the Supreme Court, which unanimously decided that the civil charges violated the clause after hearing arguments from Halper's court-appointed attorney, future chief justice John Roberts.

It also permits prosecution by different courts of law—a defendant acquitted in federal court, for example, can be prosecuted by the state government or in a civil case.

The double jeopardy clause was intended as one type of protection for individuals against government abuse. With its broad resources and power, the government could potentially pursue multiple court actions against an individual until reaching a conviction, perhaps even if the individual were innocent. A prosecutor could repeatedly attempt to

A defendant cannot be forced to testify during the trial. If he does choose to take the witness stand, though, he must answer every question regardless of self-incrimination.

convict a defendant who had been found not guilty. The ordeal could cause a defendant psychological and financial hardship.

The concept of protection against double jeopardy dates back to the Greeks and Romans. English common law included protection against double jeopardy, but it was unevenly interpreted and enforced. In cases where the crown had an interest, prosecutors could often find a justification to hold a second trial after an acquittal.

Many American colonies, beginning with Massachusetts, adopted various versions of the double jeopardy prohibition. In some instances, it was limited to allowing a defendant to plead a prior acquittal or conviction at trial. In others, any prior trial could bar a new trial regardless of outcome.

Self-Incrimination

The third clause of the Fifth Amendment prohibits the government from forcing defendants to offer testimony that might be used against them in criminal proceedings:

> . . . nor shall be compelled in any criminal case to be a witness against himself

The third clause is the best-known provision of the Fifth Amendment. When an individual "takes the Fifth" during questioning, he or she is invoking the constitutional right against self-incrimination. The protection extends only to testimony, not to personal documents or physical evidence, such as fingerprints.

One guiding principle behind the self-incrimination clause is that the government must establish its case through evidence. This is known as the accusatorial system of criminal justice. The alternative is the inquisitorial system, under which guilt is established through interrogation of the suspect under oath. Under an inquisitorial system, testimony may be coerced through torture, trickery, or threats. The self-incrimination clause of the Fifth Amendment protects the individual from possible abuse of power by the government in investigating and prosecuting criminal cases. Even police questioning is inherently coercive, as established in the case of *Miranda v. Arizona.* Therefore, police must explicitly inform a suspect of his or her right to silence under the Constitution.

Early English common law included elements of both the accusatorial and inquisitional systems. Beginning in the fourteenth century, a royal body called the Court of the Star Chamber held the authority to prosecute defendants under the inquisitional system. It often targeted political and religious dissenters. Star Chamber officials required defendants to undergo interrogation under oath, and answers were sometimes coerced by torture.

In 1637, officials arrested a young clothier's apprentice named John Lilburne, who was accused of shipping treasonous books into England. When clerks asked Lilburne to take the formal Star Chamber oath to tell the truth, he repeatedly refused but was convicted anyway. As part of his sentence, Lilburne was beaten nearly to death. His fight against forced testimony became a popular cause for discontented English subjects. In 1641, the Star Chamber was abolished and Parliament enacted the first law establishing the right against self-incrimination.

A few of the American colonies had adopted the right against self-incrimination even before the English government made it law. There has never been an American inquisitional court like the Star Chamber. Still, the right was not universally accepted, and there were occasional instances in colonial America when it became an issue in court. In 1689, in Pennsylvania, a printer named William Bradford printed copies of a pamphlet critical of John Blackwell, the deputy governor of the colony. Upon questioning, Bradford refused to confess that he had done the

John Lilburne was an early champion for social, political, and economic reforms. His fight for the right against self-incrimination caused a sensation in England.

printing. Unable to resolve the case, Blackwell resigned. Throughout the seventeenth and eighteenth century, court cases tended to strengthen the right against self-incrimination.

Due Process

The fourth clause of the Fifth Amendment states that defendants have a fundamental right to proper procedures and basic abstract concepts of justice.

> . . . nor be deprived of life, liberty, or property, without due process of law

There are two categories of due process. Procedural due process deals with the legal processes and requires that all procedures, from arrest through sentencing, must be fair. Substantive due process requires that the content of the laws themselves must be fair.

The right of due process has roots in the Magna Carta, the charter dating from 1215 that set restraints on the king of England's power. It established the basis of some legal principles that eventually were incorporated into the U.S. Constitution. The Magna Carta states, "No freeman shall be taken, or imprisoned, or disseised, or outlawed, or exiled…except by the legal judgment of his peers or by the law of the land." The due process clause similarly invokes a concept of justice similar to the "law of the land" mentioned in the Magna Carta.

In the early seventeenth century, an English judge named Edward Coke challenged the king's authority to order arrests. He held that the courts of justice, not the king, had the right to decide legal matters. In 1621, Coke was imprisoned for seven months in the Tower of London for his opposition to the king's policies. Coke's activities helped bring about the Parliament passage of a document called the Petition of Right in 1628. Among other rights, it implied a right to due process.

The American colonies adopted the right of due process to a greater extent than England did. Although the king was restricted by due process, the Parliament was not. The legal and governmental institutions developing in the American colonies, and later the United States, were limited by due process.

Just Compensation

The fifth clause in the Fifth Amendment limits the government's authority to seize private property:

In New London, Connecticut, a sign protests eminent domain seizure at one of the last structures left standing in the neighborhood that was the site of a bitter 2005 fight over property rights.

. . . nor shall private property be taken for public use, without just compensation.

This element of the Fifth Amendment is sometimes called the Takings Clause. It restricts eminent domain—the government's authority to take private property for public use. Unlike the other provisions of the amendment, this clause does not relate to criminal cases.

The same article of the Magna Carta that established due process also implied the right to just compensation. It stated that no man should be "disseised," or deprived of possessions, except by the judgment of his peers or law of the land.

The just compensation clause tries to balance public needs and private property rights. Throughout American history, the government has relied on the power of eminent domain to take land for projects such as roads, railways, and dams. Before the American Revolution, both the British and colonial governments seized private land and personal possessions without offering compensation. The just compensation clause was intended to prevent this practice from continuing in the new United States.

CHAPTER TWO

THE BILL OF RIGHTS AND THE FIFTH AMENDMENT

During the early years of American independence, the states were governed by a document called the Articles of Confederation. Though the original draft of the articles intended to create a strong federal government, the result was a loose association of states. The federal government functioned inefficiently and weakly under the articles, and problems arose among the states as they quarreled over western territory and passed laws against each other. The young nation's Congress realized that unless a stronger government came into force, the disputes would pull the country apart.

In 1787, fifty-five delegates—including leaders such as George Washington, Thomas Jefferson, and Benjamin Franklin—met in

Philadelphia for a national conference to strengthen and improve the Articles of Confederation. Of the thirteen states, only Rhode Island did not send representatives. The convention met from May 25 to September 17, 1787, and brought about radical changes to the government.

As the delegates came to realize that the Articles of Confederation would have to be replaced, intense debate broke out as they presented their ideas on the structure and powers of the new government. The delegates brought a wide range of opinions about how the new government should function, with two main factions—the Federalists and the Anti-Federalists—emerging.

Federalists such as Washington, Franklin, and Alexander Hamilton believed in having a strong central government that would have the authority to collect taxes, enforce laws, and negotiate trade agreements with other nations. The Anti-Federalists, including Thomas Jefferson and Patrick Henry, believed these and other matters should be left up to the states themselves and that establishing a strong central government would eventually lead to tyranny. The delegates had to draft a document that would satisfy both sides.

George Washington presides over the signing of the U.S. Constitution in Philadelphia on September 17, 1787. The document next went to state conventions for ratification.

During the convention, delegates studied past forms of government and drew on existing documents such as state constitutions to craft a system of government that could be agreed upon by all thirteen states. James Madison of Virginia was one of the most influential members.

He wrote a series of fifteen resolutions called the Virginia Plan that proposed sweeping changes to the federal government. The proposals included a bicameral, or two-chambered, Congress, as well as judicial and executive branches of government that would have the power to make and enforce laws. States would retain many of their powers, but they would also be part of an active national government. Madison's Virginia Plan ultimately formed the basis of the federal government. The final document largely represented the Federalist viewpoints. Federalists gained the advantage by presenting a formal plan of government by gaining the support of influential land-owning men who could vote and through persuasive arguments by famous Federalists such as Washington, Madison, and Hamilton.

The Constitution was completed and signed on September 17, 1787. The next step was for delegates to return to their states and have the document ratified, or approved, by conventions in order for it to become law. When nine of the thirteen states ratified the Constitution, it would come into force and the new government would be formed. However, even as the document headed to the states for ratification, the Federalists and Anti-Federalists continued to disagree over the new government.

Some founders worried that Anti-Federalists in state governments would refuse to support ratification unless a bill of rights was included. South Carolina delegate Charles Pinckney had first proposed a bill of rights in 1787 during the Constitutional Convention. The idea was unanimously rejected, though leaders like Thomas Jefferson later came to criticize the Constitution for not guaranteeing specific rights. These leaders wanted a bill of rights that would protect citizens and guarantee that the nation's government would never become tyrannical.

Others opposed adding a bill of rights to the Constitution. They felt that if they added a list of amendments to the Constitution, the

Federalist James Madison is widely known as the father of the Constitution and as the author of the Bill of Rights. He was elected president of the United States in 1808.

document's protections would be limited only to those specific rights. In 1787, Hamilton, Madison, and John Jay began publishing a series of eighty-five essays that attempted to explain why the Constitution was needed. The Federalist Papers, as the essays came to be called, specifically argued against a bill of rights.

The articles by Hamilton, Madison, and Jay helped generate support for ratifying the Constitution, but they did not calm the anxieties of the Anti-Federalists. Ratification of the Constitution came to hinge on approving a bill of rights. Massachusetts, Virginia, New Hampshire, and New York agreed to ratify the document only if their delegates could recommend amendments. North Carolina refused to ratify the Constitution unless progress was made on drafting a bill of rights.

The Due Process Amendments

The amendments that make up the Bill of Rights—including the Fifth Amendment—were drawn up to protect the rights of U.S. citizens from actions taken by the federal government. However, the due process protections offered by the Fifth Amendment did not extend to actions taken by the states. This left citizens vulnerable to actions by state governments that would be considered unconstitutional if they were carried out by the federal government. In 1868, shortly after the end of the Civil War (1861–1865), the states ratified the Fourteenth Amendment to the Constitution as a way to guarantee that former slaves would be granted their rights as citizens. It made most of the Fifth's protections applicable to the states by declaring that states cannot deprive "any person of life, liberty, or property, without due process of law; nor deny to any person within its jurisdiction the equal protection of the laws." However, the due process protections were granted only on a case-by-case basis due to evolving interpretations of what "due process" meant. By the 1960s, the Supreme Court had extended nearly every provision of the Bill of Rights to the states.

Drafting the Amendments

James Madison had not believed that a bill of rights was needed. However, he decided that he would support a bill of rights if it were necessary to guarantee ratification of the Constitution. Madison himself took up the work of drafting the document. He began by taking suggestions from other leaders who felt that individual rights needed to be protected. Madison also looked to various contemporary and historical sources for inspiration.

The Virginia Declaration of Rights was one of the documents he consulted. George Mason wrote the Virginia Declaration of Rights in 1776 as the American colonies were breaking away from Great Britain. Mason used the English Bill of Rights as a model in drafting his document, which outlined the rights to life, liberty, and property. The Virginia Declaration of Rights also included some of the specific clauses that later became part of the Fifth Amendment. These included the right to remain silent and the due process clause. After the Revolutionary War, Mason became one of the delegates to the Constitutional Convention who refused to sign the document because it did not contain a bill of rights.

In formulating the Fifth Amendment, Madison drew on a variety of sources in addition to the Virginia Declaration of Rights, including state constitutions and proposals by state-ratifying conventions. He even scoured newspapers for opinions on proposed amendments. All the clauses that make up the Fifth Amendment had precedent in the American colonies, although not every right was accepted by every colony.

The Path Toward Ratification

To create the final document, Madison condensed the ideas that he collected from other leaders and gathered from existing documents. On

NUMBER XXXIX.

The Conformity of the Plan to Republican Principles : An Objection in Respect to the Powers of the Convention, examined.

THE last paper having concluded the observations which were meant to introduce a candid survey of the plan of government reported by the convention, we now proceed to the execution of that part of our undertaking. The first question that offers itself is, whether the general form and aspect of the government be strictly republican? It is evident that no other form would be reconcileable with the genius of the people of America; with the fundamental principles of the revolution ; or with that honorable determination, which animates every votary of freedom, to rest all our political experiments on the capacity of mankind for self-government. If the plan of the convention therefore be found to depart from the republican character, its advocates must abandon it as no longer defensible.

What then are the distinctive characters of the republican form? Were an answer to this question to be sought, not by recurring to principles, but in the application of the term by political writers, to the constitutions of different states, no satisfactory one would ever be found. Holland, in which no particle of the supreme authority is derived from the people, has passed almost universally under the denomination of a republic. The same title has been bestowed on Venice, where absolute power over the great body of the people, is exercised in the most absolute manner, by a small body of hereditary nobles. Poland, which is a mixture of aristocracy and of monarchy in their worst forms, has been dignified with the same appellation. The government of England, which has one republican branch

branch only, combined with a hereditary aristocracy and monarchy, has with equal impropriety been frequently placed on the list of republics. These examples, which are nearly as dissimilar to each other as to a genuine republic, shew the extreme inaccuracy with which the term has been used in political disquisitions.

If we resort for a criterion, to the different principles on which different forms of government are established, we may define a republic to be, or at least may bestow that name on, a government which derives all its powers directly or indirectly from the great body of the people ; and is administered by persons holding their offices during pleasure, for a limited period, or during good behaviour. It is *essential* to such a government, that it be derived from the great body of the society, not from an inconsiderable proportion, or a favored class of it ; otherwise a handful of tyrannical nobles, exercising their oppressions by a delegation of their powers, might aspire to the rank of republicans, and claim for their government the honorable title of republic. It is *sufficient* for such a government, that the persons administering it be appointed, either directly or indirectly, by the people ; and that they hold their appointments by either of the tenures just specified ; otherwise every government in the United States, as well as every other popular government that has been or can be well organised or well executed, would be degraded from the republican character. According to the constitution of every state in the union, some or other of the officers of government are appointed indirectly only by the people. According to most of them the chief magistrate himself is so appointed. And according to one, this mode of appointment is extended to one of the co-ordinate branches of the legislature. According to all the constitutions also, the tenure of the highest offices is extended to a definite period, and in many instances, both within the legislative and executive departments, to a period of

In the Federalist Papers, written during 1787 and 1788, Madison, Hamilton, and Jay put forth sophisticated and compelling arguments in support of ratifying the Constitution.

June 8, 1789, he presented these ideas to Congress as a bill of rights amending the Constitution. Congress approved twelve of the amendments on September 25, 1789.

Upon review by House and Senate members, there was little opposition to the principles put forth in the Fifth Amendment. The grand jury clause and due process clause were accepted with no opposition. The double jeopardy clause, self-incrimination clause, and just compensation clause were altered slightly from Madison's original wording.

Madison's original version of the double jeopardy clause read, "No person shall be subject, except in cases of impeachment, to more than one punishment or trial for the same offense." There were objections to

THE BILL OF RIGHTS AND THE FIFTH AMENDMENT | 29

the phrasing. Some people pointed out that if a defendant judged guilty appealed the ruling, the amendment could be interpreted to prohibit a second trial, potentially allowing a guilty defendant to go free.

The first version of Madison's self-incrimination clause included the phrasing "nor shall be compelled to be a witness against himself." The phrase "in any criminal case" was added later.

Madison's early version of the just compensation clause read, "nor be obliged to relinquish his property, where it may be necessary for public use, without a just compensation." The final wording was altered slightly, but the meaning remained unchanged.

The approved Bill of Rights was then sent out to the states to be ratified. The ratification process for the Constitution, which began in 1787 and was completed in 1788, had been rocky and involved bitter arguments between the Federalists and Anti-Federalists. By the time Madison started drafting the Bill of Rights in 1789, the Constitution had been ratified by eleven of the thirteen states and the new government was in place, with Washington as president. While there were some heated debates over ratifying the Bill of Rights, the process was not as contentious as the ratification of the Constitution.

In order for the amendments to become law, they had to be ratified by ten of the thirteen states. Of the twelve amendments that had been proposed, two failed the ratification process. On November 20, 1789, New Jersey became the first state to ratify the Bill of Rights. The process was completed on December 15, 1791, when Virginia became the tenth state to ratify the Bill of Rights and the document went into effect.

CHAPTER THREE

IMPACT OF THE FIFTH AMENDMENT

Before the adoption of the Bill of Rights, the various colonies—
and later, states—had adopted a patchwork of different rights in
their charters and constitutions. After the American Revolution,
most states drafted new constitutions, although not all states included
a bill of rights. The structure and content of these constitutions var-
ied widely. Every state guaranteed the right to trial by jury. All but
four states established the right against self-incrimination. Only New
Hampshire included a mention of double jeopardy. None of the states
had a constitutional guarantee of due process or just compensation.

After the Constitution was ratified, every state was required to
respect the liberties listed in the Bill of Rights. Moreover, officials

associated with the legal system had to agree on an interpretation of the text of the amendments. The framers of the Constitution had tried to convey their intentions clearly and specifically, but they were dealing with abstract and complicated issues. For example, regarding the self-incrimination clause, is a confession "compelled" or voluntary if the defendant is tricked into answering? How wide is the scope of "due process of law"? What constitutes "public use" in the just compensation clause—does the land have to be publicly owned, or merely accessible to the public?

Throughout the centuries since the adoption of the Bill of Rights, court rulings have clarified the scope and limitations of the amendments. Today, when a judge is considering a difficult case, he or she will examine similar cases from the past that set applicable legal precedents. Some of these cases, such as *Miranda v. Arizona*, ushered in a whole new judicial era. Many other cases, however, clarified more minor points of law. Occasional cases bring the reversal of a precedent, since prevailing legal opinions on some points have shifted over the years.

Grand Jury

The framers of the Constitution held the institution of the grand jury in very high esteem. For them, politically motivated prosecutions were recent history. Through its impartiality, the grand jury served an important role in protecting the rights of the accused from overreaching government authority.

Today, grand juries still fulfill an important function in the justice system, but their part in reining in prosecutors may have waned. Grand juries vote to indict in a significant majority of cases, perhaps because ordinary citizens are unwilling to challenge a prosecutor's expertise. The grand jury clause of the Fifth Amendment has not been extended to

States are not required to use grand juries in order to indict. In some cases, the prosecutor will simply present evidence directly to a judge.

state governments. Some states indict through a grand jury system. But in many, the prosecutor presents a formal statement of charges directly to a judge.

This precedent dates back to the 1884 case of *Hurtado v. California*. Convicted of murder, Joseph Hurtado appealed the ruling on the basis that he had not been indicted by a grand jury. This, he claimed, violated his right to due process, since the Fourteenth Amendment guaranteed his right to a grand jury in a state court. The U.S. Supreme Court disagreed, ruling that the conviction was justified. One argument was that since the grand jury clause had not been explicitly included in the Fourteenth Amendment, the grand jury provision did not apply to the states.

Double Jeopardy

Although the meaning of the double jeopardy clause appears straightforward, interpretation has proven a challenge for legal experts. The problems begin with defining "same offense." When committing a crime, a criminal may break multiple laws. Can the defendant be tried for the multiple offenses committed? Or does the phrase "same offense" mean that a prosecutor must choose to pursue a single offense violating a single law?

A Supreme Court ruling in the 1932 case *Blockburger v. United States* introduced a means of determining whether or not a defendant can be charged with multiple offenses without violating double jeopardy. It is called the Blockburger, or "same elements," test. Justice George Sutherland wrote, "The test to be applied to determine whether there are two offenses or only one is whether each provision requires proof of an additional fact which the other does not." In other words, a prosecutor can prosecute only one crime from a set of evidence. If the crime investigation yields multiple sets of evidence pointing to multiple crimes, though, the prosecutor can prosecute multiple crimes. For instance, if a man assaulted a homeowner during a burglary, different evidence would

be presented during a prosecution for assault than during a prosecution for burglary. In later cases, the Supreme Court would change the focus of the test to the defendant's conduct, rather than evidence.

One example of the Blockburger test put to use is the 1977 case

Brown v. Ohio. The defendant was put on trial twice for offenses involving the same incident. He was convicted first of joyriding and then convicted a second time for stealing the automobile that he had been driving at the time. Since identical evidence had been used to obtain both convictions, the Supreme Court overturned the second conviction on the grounds that it constituted double jeopardy.

According to the double jeopardy clause, a defendant cannot be retried after acquittal. (One rare exception was a case where the defendant bribed the judge. Since the defendant was never in jeopardy, due to the bribe, a second prosecution does not qualify as double jeopardy.) In some circumstances, however, a defendant can be prosecuted a second time in case of mistrial. There are also instances in which a defendant can receive a second trial after a conviction. If a defendant appeals a conviction and it is overturned by the appeals court, a second trial may be allowed, such as when the reversal was due to trial error.

A police officer collects evidence to be used in a 2005 murder case in New York. There were both a criminal trial and civil actions related to the case.

Self-Incrimination

To most people, the Fifth Amendment is embodied in the Miranda warning, which begins, "You have the right to remain silent; anything you say can and will be used against you in a court of law." It is a standard piece of police procedure—before being questioned, a suspect in custody must be informed of his or her constitutional rights. The right against self-incrimination extends beyond custodial questioning, however. Defendants can refuse to testify in court on the grounds of self-incrimination. Witnesses called to testify at another person's trial can claim the right against self-incrimination in refusing to answer specific questions.

A defendant can only "take the Fifth" on the grounds of self-incrimination. He or she cannot refuse to answer for other reasons, such as embarrassment. The defendant cannot take the Fifth in refusing to incriminate another person. Only an individual can invoke the right against self-incrimination—an organization such as a corporation cannot take the Fifth.

The right against self-incrimination is often discussed in conjunction with due process, since some methods of coercing confession violate principles of due process. It is also linked to the idea that a defendant is assumed innocent until proven guilty. Proof of guilt must come through evidence, not forced confessions. In addition, the right against self-incrimination is related to the right to privacy from government intrusion.

During the early and mid-twentieth century, several court rulings significantly broadened the applications of the privilege against self-incrimination. It took a long time for the right to be extended to the states. The 1908 Supreme Court ruling in *Twining v. New Jersey* held that the right against self-incrimination was not one of the principles of due process and therefore did not apply to state governments. In 1936, the Supreme Court heard the case of *Brown v. Mississippi*. Three black men had been convicted of the murder of a white farmer. The police had beaten and tortured them into confession, and the convictions were based solely on the confessions. The Court overturned the convictions on the basis that the forced confessions and the use of the confessions in court violated due process. They did not, however, extend the right against self-incrimination to the states in the ruling. Finally, in 1964, the Supreme Court ruled in the case of *Malloy v. Hogan* that the self-incrimination clause did apply to the states because, otherwise, federal and state courts would hold two different standards of judgment.

During this period, the Supreme Court issued a number of rulings examining whether confessions were truly voluntary and thus admissible in court. Confessions obtained through techniques such as lengthy inter-rogations and psychological coercion were ruled inadmissible. Finally, the ruling in the *Miranda v. Arizona* case in 1966 required that any suspect in custody be informed of his or her Fifth Amendment rights.

When a defendant in a criminal trial takes the Fifth and refuses to testify, it does not qualify as an admission of guilt. The defendant can request that the judge instruct the jury not to take an inference of guilt from a refusal to testify. The prosecutor is not permitted to argue before the jury that a defendant's silence indicates guilt.

The right against self-incrimination does not apply when a witness is granted immunity by the government. An individual may be given immunity from prosecution when he or she testifies before a body, such as a grand jury or legislative committee, during an investigation. A refusal to answer may be considered criminal contempt of court.

In 1987, congressional committees were established to investigate the Iran-Contra affair, a government scandal involving illegally sold

Lieutenant Colonel Oliver North is sworn in before a congressional committee hearing in 1986. North's immunized testimony could not be used as evidence in his 1989 prosecution.

arms. Lieutenant Colonel Oliver North was granted immunity, and he offered extensive testimony during the hearings. Two years later, North was prosecuted and convicted on three criminal violations related to the scandal. The convictions were later reversed because they relied on his testimony given under immunity.

Due Process

The due process clause establishes that the government must act with fairness in depriving people of "life, liberty, or property." Due process is an abstract concept, so judges often disagree on the correct interpretation. One viewpoint is that consideration of due process should be closely restricted to its original scope under English common law. This would tend to limit it to legal procedures. The opposite viewpoint is that due process reflects standards of fairness, which may evolve over time.

The Fifth and Fourteenth amendments both guarantee the right of due process. Most key due process court cases have involved local or state matters, which concern the Fourteenth, rather than the Fifth, Amendment. In 1954, a Supreme Court ruling struck down racially segregated schools in the landmark case *Brown v. Board of Education of Topeka*. The basis was that segregated schools violated rights in the Fourteenth Amendment. In a companion ruling issued the same day, *Bolling v. Sharpe*, the Court struck down racially segregated schools in Washington, D.C. Since Washington, D.C., is a federal city, the Court justified the opinion using the due process clause of the Fifth Amendment.

The case *Bolling v. Sharpe* involves substantive due process, since it addresses the content of a law. The other type of due process, procedural due process, deals with the procedures that the law moves through.

The Right to Remain Silent and the McCarthy Era

A wave of anti-communist hysteria hit the United States beginning in February 1950, after Senator Joseph McCarthy of Wisconsin alleged in several speeches that communist operatives were working in the State Department. State and federal legislative committees were formed to investigate communist subversion in many aspects of American life, including the government, the education system, and the entertainment industry. People accused of having communist sympathies were called before these committees to answer questions about their beliefs, activities, and associations. Their testimony could make them vulnerable to state and federal laws against conspiring to overthrow the government. People who were called to testify were entitled to refuse to answer questions on Fifth Amendment grounds. However, those who refused to testify were labeled "Fifth Amendment Communists" on the basis that by not answering questions, they must be hiding something. The committees often damaged the lives, reputations, and careers of those called to testify, regardless of the truth of the accusations made. Some, like famed playwright Arthur Miller, had to pay steep fines. Others went to prison. The hysteria of the McCarthy Era did not begin subsiding until 1954, when McCarthy lost credibility by accusing high-ranking members of the armed forces of having communist connections.

Just Compensation

The just compensation clause protects a property owner's rights by restricting the government's power of eminent domain. When the government seizes private property for public use, it is known as a taking. The just compensation clause requires that the government compensate, or pay, the property owner.

The first Supreme Court case ever to address the Bill of Rights involved a property owner demanding just compensation. In the 1833 ruling on *Barron v. Baltimore*, the Court found that the city of Baltimore did not have to pay for damages done to private property during construction. The basis for the decision was that the Bill of Rights did not extend to the states. In 1897, however, the Supreme Court ruled in the case of *Chicago, Burlington and Quincy Railroad Company v. Chicago* that due process did require that states offer just compensation for takings.

Subsequent Supreme Court rulings have clarified the definitions in the just compensation clause. What constitutes a "taking"? What "public use" justifies government seizure of private property?

A taking is the physical takeover of private property, such as when the government demolishes a house to make way for a freeway. In some cases, property owners have argued that a government restriction on the use of private property also constitutes a taking. Zoning laws or environmental regulations, for example, limit how an owner can develop property. If these laws cause a loss in value of the property, the government should offer just compensation for the loss. This expanded view on takings would further restrict the government power of eminent domain.

In the 1978 case *Penn Central Transportation Company v. City of New York*, the Supreme Court rejected one such argument that would have broadened the scope of the just compensation clause. Penn Central Transportation Company planned to build a high-rise office building on top of Grand Central Station. New York's Landmarks Preservation Commission blocked construction, since it would have considerably altered a historic site. The Supreme Court ruled that the Landmarks Preservation Law did not deprive them of their property and did not qualify as a taking.

Decisions involving the just compensation clause often prove controversial to the general public. Here, protesters mark the anniversary of the unpopular 2005 *Kelo v. City of New London* verdict.

In rulings on acceptable "public use," the Supreme Court has tended to defer to state legislation. For example, in 1984, the Court heard the case of *Hawaii Housing Authority v. Midkiff.* The Hawaii Land Reform Act aimed to reduce concentrated land ownership. The Supreme Court ruled that requiring some private owners to sell their land to other private individuals was acceptable because it served a public purpose.

In *Lucas v. South Carolina Coastal Council*, a major 1992 takings case, however, the Supreme Court ruled on the side of the property owner. A new state law allowed the coastal council to prohibit new construction on oceanfront lots. David Lucas sued, since the new law made his property worthless. The Court found that the new law qualified as a taking and that Lucas should be fairly compensated.

CHAPTER FOUR

THE FIFTH AMENDMENT TODAY

The Fifth Amendment is an important element in shaping how justice—and the justice system—works in the United States today. Because of the Fifth Amendment, citizens are secure in the knowledge that they live in a nation with fair laws that are fairly administered. The Fifth Amendment impacts how the police investigate crimes and how lawyers prosecute and defend defendants. Property owners do not have to fear that they will be deprived of their homes and financial security by the government's power of eminent domain.

Nonetheless, the Fifth Amendment continues to adapt to changing times and shifting legal philosophies. Contemporary interpretation of

Juvenile offenders await testing and evaluation at a Texas facility. Juveniles are entitled to due process of the law as well as many other Fifth Amendment protections.

the Fifth Amendment is based on legal precedents set by hundreds of cases. Into the twenty-first century, the Supreme Court continues to hand down important rulings on the Fifth Amendment that confirm, clarify, or even reverse past decisions.

As a young adult, however, you may not see the relevance of the Fifth Amendment in your daily life. Most adolescents don't spend much time pondering legal procedures, property rights, and the theoretical underpinning of the nation's laws. Nonetheless, one of the groundbreaking Supreme Court rulings of the twentieth century involved a case brought by a teenage boy. The case, *In re Gault,* transformed the way the U.S. juvenile justice system works.

Until the twentieth century, juvenile offenders were treated much like adults. They could be given long sentences that would be served in a prison alongside adults, not in a facility for juveniles. Reformers developed an independent juvenile justice system intended to rehabilitate young offenders. The government began taking on a parental, rather than disciplinary, role regarding juveniles. As a result, many of the procedures and protections available to adults were denied to juveniles.

In 1964, fifteen-year-old Gerald Gault was taken into custody for making obscene phone calls to a neighbor. His parents were not informed of his detention and upcoming hearing, and the neighbor did not testify in court. There were no transcripts of the proceedings. After the hearing, the judge ordered Gault committed to the state reform school until he turned twenty-one. Gault appealed the case. Eventually, the Supreme Court overturned the conviction in 1967. The Court ruled in *In re Gault* that juveniles had a right to due process and many constitutional protections guaranteed in the Bill of Rights, including the right against self-incrimination granted in the Fifth Amendment.

Amendment in Action: Kelo v. City of New London

One of the most unpopular Supreme Court rulings in recent times was the 2005 verdict in the case *Kelo v. City of New London*. The economically depressed city of New London, Connecticut, proposed to revitalize its economy by encouraging private development. The city bought private land for the purpose, but some owners refused to sell. The city then used its power of eminent domain to condemn and seize the properties. Susette Kelo sued, claiming that selling the property to a private development company did not constitute "public use." The Supreme Court held that the taking was justified on the grounds that it would promote economic development. Therefore, it served a "public purpose."

The verdict resulted in public outrage. Members of Congress from both parties protested the decision. Dozens of states enacted new legislation prohibiting the use of eminent domain for economic development. Although the ruling did not break any new legal ground, the public reaction demonstrated the value that Americans place on property rights and the importance of the just compensation clause of the Fifth Amendment in protecting those rights.

Reversing Course

In issuing rulings, the Supreme Court frequently reverses decisions made by lower courts. Sometimes, though, it reverses previous Supreme Court rulings. The extension of Fifth Amendment provisions to the states reversed past rulings that denied that the rights applied to state governments.

Another example of the Supreme Court reversing a past ruling dealt with part of the grand jury clause. Members of the military are excluded from the right to indictment by a grand jury. In 1969, in the case *O'Callahan v. Parker*, the Supreme Court heard the case of a service member who had been court-martialed in a military tribunal for a crime he had

A 2004 Supreme Court ruling found that enemy combatants may challenge their detainment under due process. Here, a military courtroom in Guantánamo Bay, Cuba, has been prepared for possible trials.

committed off base. The crime had not been service-connected. The Court found that the military tribunal had overstepped its jurisdiction and the service member was entitled to a trial in civilian courts, which would grant him the right to a grand jury or a trial by jury. In 1987, the Court heard the similar case *Solorio v. United States.* This time, the Court overruled *O'Callahan v. Parker.* The ruling stated that a crime committed during military service did not have to be service-connected in order to fall under the jurisdiction of a military tribunal.

After *Miranda*

Stark reversals of previous rulings are rare. More often, when the Supreme Court revisits an issue, the new ruling merely clarifies or limits a previous ruling. This has occurred numerous times in cases related to the Miranda warning.

Although the guidelines on issuing the Miranda were straightforward, ambiguities emerged. What constituted "custody"? A later ruling clarified that a suspect deprived of his or her freedom of action must be read the Miranda warning, whether at a police station or elsewhere. In 1977, however, the Court ruled that an Internal Revenue Service (IRS) agent informally questioning a man at his home did not violate

A routine traffic stop is not legally considered to be custodial interrogation, so police officers are not required to read the Miranda warning to drivers.

his Fifth Amendment rights, even though he was the subject of a criminal investigation. Interrogation at a police station does not qualify as being in custody without a formal arrest or restraint on freedom of movement. Routine traffic stops do not amount to custody.

Also, the original *Miranda v. Arizona* ruling did not specifically define "interrogation." Later rulings found that even if there is no direct questioning, the "functional equivalent," such as conversation intended to draw out an incriminating response, qualifies as interrogation.

Rulings made since the original 1966 decision have imposed exceptions and limitations to *Miranda*. In 1984, in the case *New York v. Quarles*, the Court created a public safety exception. A suspect carrying a gun entered a supermarket, and when a police officer spotted him and frisked him, he found an empty gun holster. The police officer demanded that the suspect tell what he had done with the gun. The Supreme Court ruled that "the gun is over there" was admissible in court, even though the officer had not issued a Miranda warning. Concern for public safety outweighed the necessity of immediately issuing the Miranda warning.

The Supreme Court continues to revisit *Miranda*. In 2003, it heard the case of *Chavez v. Martinez*. Police officer Ben Chavez interrogated Oliverio Martinez, who was at the hospital having just been shot, without issuing the Miranda warning. Martinez claimed that his right against self-incrimination and his right against coercive questioning had been violated. The Court found that Chavez did not violate the Fifth Amendment rights of Martinez because Martinez was never charged with a crime and his answers were not used against him in a criminal case. The Court did not address whether or not his due process rights had been violated.

Property Rights Battles

American citizens have a high regard for the rights of property owners. Many people resent the government's power of eminent domain and are not pacified by legal claims that government seizure of private property is for the public benefit.

New laws and restrictions concerning private property tend to lead to court challenges on whether the regulations violate a property owner's rights. In a 1994 case, *Dolan v. City of Tigard*, the Supreme Court heard Florence Dolan's claim that the city of Tigard, Oregon, violated her rights under the just compensation clause of the Fifth Amendment. Dolan had applied for a permit to expand her store and pave a parking lot. The city conditionally approved the request, requiring Dolan to dedicate part of her land to public use: a bike path and a greenway. The Court ruled that Dolan's Fifth Amendment rights had been violated, since the traffic improvements and environmental benefits did not justify the dedication of land.

In ruling on just compensation cases, the Supreme Court must balance the rights of property owners against the public good. Many of the clauses in the Fifth Amendment require such a balancing act. American citizens have the right against self-incrimination and double jeopardy. They have the right to live under a fair justice system that administers legal procedures fairly. On the other hand, it is the responsibility of the government to investigate crimes and prosecute criminals. The Supreme Court's interpretation of the Fifth Amendment ensures that Americans live in a society dedicated both to the defense of personal liberties and the pursuit of justice.

AMENDMENTS TO THE U.S. CONSTITUTION

First Amendment (proposed 1789; ratified 1791): Freedom of religion, speech, press, assembly, and petition

Second Amendment (proposed 1789; ratified 1791): Right to bear arms

Third Amendment (proposed 1789; ratified 1791): No quartering of soldiers in private houses in times of peace

Fourth Amendment (proposed 1789; ratified 1791): Interdiction of unreasonable search and seizure; requirement of search warrants

Fifth Amendment (proposed 1789; ratified 1791): Indictments; due process; self-incrimination; double jeopardy; eminent domain

Sixth Amendment (proposed 1789; ratified 1791): Right to a fair and speedy public trial; notice of accusations; confronting one's accuser; subpoenas; right to counsel

Seventh Amendment (proposed 1789; ratified 1791): Right to a trial by jury in civil cases

Eighth Amendment (proposed 1789; ratified 1791): No excessive bail and fines; no cruel or unusual punishment

Ninth Amendment (proposed 1789; ratified 1791): Protection of unenumerated rights (rights inferred from other legal rights but that are not themselves coded or enumerated in a written constitution and laws)

Tenth Amendment (proposed 1789; ratified 1791): Limits the power of the federal government

Eleventh Amendment (proposed 1794; ratified 1795): Sovereign immunity (immunity of states from suits brought by out-of-state citizens and foreigners living outside of states' borders)

Twelfth Amendment (proposed 1803; ratified 1804): Revision of presidential election procedures (electoral college)

Thirteenth Amendment (proposed 1865; ratified 1865): Abolition of slavery

Fourteenth Amendment (proposed 1866; ratified 1868): Citizenship; state due process; application of Bill of Rights to states; revision to apportionment of congressional representatives; denies public office to anyone who has rebelled against the United States

Fifteenth Amendment (proposed 1869; ratified 1870): Suffrage no longer restricted by race

Sixteenth Amendment (proposed 1909; ratified 1913): Allows federal income tax

Seventeenth Amendment (proposed 1912; ratified 1913): Direct election to the U.S. Senate by popular vote

Eighteenth Amendment (proposed 1917; ratified 1919): Prohibition of alcohol

Nineteenth Amendment (proposed 1919; ratified 1920): Women's suffrage

Twentieth Amendment (proposed 1932; ratified 1933): Term commencement for Congress (January 3) and president (January 20)

Twenty-first Amendment (proposed 1933; ratified 1933): Repeal of Eighteenth Amendment (Prohibition)

Twenty-second Amendment (proposed 1947; ratified 1951): Limits president to two terms

Twenty-third Amendment (proposed 1960; ratified 1961): Representation of Washington, D.C., in electoral college

Twenty-fourth Amendment (proposed 1962; ratified 1964): Prohibition of restriction of voting rights due to nonpayment of poll taxes

Twenty-fifth Amendment (proposed 1965; ratified 1967): Presidential succession

Twenty-sixth Amendment (proposed 1971; ratified 1971): Voting age of eighteen

Twenty-seventh Amendment (proposed 1789; ratified 1992): Congressional compensation

Proposed but Unratified Amendments

Congressional Apportionment Amendment (proposed 1789; still technically pending): Apportionment of U.S. representatives

Titles of Nobility Amendment (proposed 1810; still technically pending): Prohibition of titles of nobility

Corwin Amendment (proposed 1861; still technically pending though superseded by Thirteenth Amendment): Preservation of slavery

Child Labor Amendment (proposed 1924; still technically pending): Congressional power to regulate child labor

Equal Rights Amendment (proposed 1972; expired): Prohibition of inequality of men and women

District of Columbia Voting Rights Amendment (proposed 1978; expired): District of Columbia voting rights

GLOSSARY

acquit To declare not guilty of an offense or crime.

amendment A change or an addition to a document, such as a bill or constitution.

appeal To apply for the transfer of a case to a higher court for a new hearing.

assembly A body of elected political representatives, usually the lower house of a state legislature.

bicameral Having two branches, chambers, or houses as a legislative body.

Bill of Rights The first ten amendments added to the U.S. Constitution in 1791 that protect basic rights and liberties.

clause An article or stipulation in a document text, such as an amendment.

colony A group of people who leave their native country to form a settlement in a new land that remains subject to or connected with the parent nation.

convention A meeting or formal gathering of representatives or delegates to discuss and act on matters of common concern.

convict To find guilty of an offense or crime.

custody The state of being held by the police.

defendant The party against whom a claim or charge is brought in a court.

delegate A person chosen to act for or represent others.

eminent domain The power of the government to seize private property for public use.

federal Pertaining to a central government.

grand jury A group of citizens gathered together to consider a prosecutor's evidence and decide if a defendant should be indicted.

immunity Exemption from prosecution, often granted in exchange for testimony.

indict To formally accuse of a crime.

Parliament The legislature of Great Britain.

precedent A judicial decision that may be used as a standard in deciding similar cases in the future.

prosecute To initiate and conduct legal proceedings against in court.

ratify To confirm by expressing approval or consent.

self-incrimination The act of testifying to crimes against oneself.

testify To declare or affirm facts under oath, usually in court.

FOR MORE INFORMATION

American Constitution Society for Law and Policy
1333 H Street NW, 11th Floor
Washington, DC 20005
(202) 393-6181
Web site: http://www.acslaw.org
The American Constitution Society for Law and Policy promotes the vitality of the
U.S. Constitution and the fundamental values it expresses.

Bill of Rights Institute
200 North Glebe Road, Suite 200
Arlington, VA 22203
(703) 894-1776
Web site: http://www.billofrightsinstitute.org
The Bill of Rights Institute's mission is to educate young people about the words and
ideas of America's founders and the liberties guaranteed in founding documents.

Canadian Bar Association (CBA)
500–865 Carling Avenue
Ottawa, ON K1S 5S8
Canada
(613) 237-2925
Web site: http://www.cba.org
The CBA is the organization made up of members of Canada's legal profession.

National Constitution Center
Independence Mall
525 Arch Street

Philadelphia, PA 19106
(215) 409-6600
Web site: http://constitutioncenter.org
The National Constitution Center is dedicated to promoting a better understanding
of and appreciation for the Constitution, its history, and its contemporary relevance.

Parliament of Canada
Information Service
Ottawa, ON K1A 0A9
Canada
(613) 992-4793
Web site: http://www.parl.gc.ca
The Canadian Parliament was established in 1867 and serves as the nation's legislative
body. It is modeled after the British Parliament.

U.S. National Archives and Records Administration
8601 Adelphi Road
College Park, MD 20740
(866) 272-6272
Web site: http://www.archives.gov
The U.S. National Archives and Records Administration preserves government documents and records that have historical or legal significance.

Web Sites

Due to the changing nature of Internet links, Rosen Publishing has
developed an online list of Web sites related to the subject of this book.
This site is updated regularly. Please use this link to access the list:

http://www.rosenlinks.com/ausc/5th

FOR FURTHER READING

Armentrout, David, and Patricia Armentrout. *The Bill of Rights*. Vero Beach, FL: Rourke Publishing, 2005.

Finkelman, Paul, ed. *Milestone Documents in American History: Exploring the Primary Sources That Shaped America*. Dallas, TX: Schlager Group, 2008.

Fridell, Ron. *Miranda Law: The Right to Remain Silent*. New York, NY: Marshall Cavendish Benchmark, 2006.

Graham, Amy. *A Look at the Bill of Rights: Protecting the Rights of Americans*. Berkeley Heights, NJ: Enslow Publishers, 2008.

Hall, Kermit, ed. *The Oxford Companion to the Supreme Court of the United States*. 2nd ed. New York, NY: Oxford University Press, 2005.

Hall, Kermit, ed. *The Oxford Guide to United States Supreme Court Decisions*. 2nd ed. New York, NY: Oxford University Press, 2009.

Harper, Timothy. *The Complete Idiot's Guide to the U.S. Constitution*. Indianapolis, IN: Alpha Books, 2007.

Hennessey, Jonathan. *The United States Constitution: A Graphic Adaptation*. New York, NY: Hill and Wang, 2008.

Labunkski, Richard. *James Madison and the Struggle for the Bill of Rights*. New York, NY: Oxford University Press, 2006.

Leavitt, Amie Jane. *The Bill of Rights in Translation: What It Really Means*. Mankato, MN: Capstone Press, 2009.

Nardo, Don, ed. *The Creation of the U.S. Constitution: Opposing Viewpoints*. Detroit, MI: Greenhaven Press, 2005.

Nelson, Robin. *Constitution Day*. Minneapolis, MN: Lerner Publications, 2010.

Panchyk, Richard. *Our Supreme Court*. Chicago, IL: Chicago Review Press, 2007.

Smith, Rich. *Fifth Amendment: The Right to Fairness*. Edina, MN: ABDO Publishing, 2008.

Smith, Rich. *How Amendments Are Adopted*. Edina, MN: ABDO Publishing, 2009.

Sobel, Syl. *The Bill of Rights: Protecting Our Freedom Then and Now*. Hauppauge, NY: Barrons Educational Series, 2008.

Spagenburg, Ray, and Kit Moser. *Civil Liberties*. Tarrytown, NY: Marshall Cavendish Benchmark, 2006.

Thomas, William David. *What Is a Constitution?* Pleasantville, NY: Gareth Stevens Publishing, 2008.

Truly, Traci. *Teen Rights (and Responsibilities): A Legal Guide for Teens and the Adults in Their Lives*. Naperville, IL: Sphinx Publications, 2005.

Yero, Judith Lloyd. *The Bill of Rights*. Washington, DC: National Geographic, 2006.

BIBLIOGRAPHY

Congressional Research Service. "CRS Annotated Constitution." Retrieved April 15, 2010 (http://www.law.cornell.edu/anncon/index.html).

Cook, Don. *The Long Fuse: How England Lost the American Colonies, 1760–1785*. New York, NY: Atlantic Monthly Press, 1995.

FindLaw. *Blockburger v. United States*. Retrieved April 15, 2010 (http://laws.findlaw.com/us/284/299.html).

FindLaw. *Chavez v. Martinez*. Retrieved April 15, 2010 (http://laws.findlaw.com/us/000/01-1444.html).

FindLaw. *Dolan v. City of Tigard*. Retrieved April 15, 2010 (http://laws.findlaw.com/us/512/374.html).

FindLaw. *Kelo v. City of New London*. Retrieved April 15, 2010 (http://laws.findlaw.com/us/000/04-108.html).

FindLaw. *Penn Central Transportation Company v. City of New York*. Retrieved April 15, 2010 (http://laws.findlaw.com/us/438/104.html).

FindLaw. *United States v. Halper*. Retrieved April 15, 2010 (http://laws.findlaw.com/us/490/435.html).

Fireside, Harvey. *The Fifth Amendment: The Right to Remain Silent*. Berkeley Heights, NJ: Enslow Publishers, 1998.

Holder, Angela Roddey, and John Thomas Roddey Holder. *The Meaning of the Constitution*. 3rd ed. Hauppage, NY: Barron's Educational Series, 1997.

Levy, Leonard W. *Origins of the Fifth Amendment: The Right Against Self-Incrimination*. Chicago, IL: Ivan R. Dee, 1999.

Levy, Leonard W., ed. *Essays on the Making of the Constitution*. 2nd ed. New York, NY: Oxford University Press, 1987.

Mauro, Tony. *Illustrated Great Decisions of the Supreme Court.* Washington, DC: CQ Press, 2000.

Mitchell, Ralph. *CQ's Guide to the U.S. Constitution.* Washington, DC: Congressional Quarterly, 1994.

Monk, Linda R. *The Words We Live By: Your Annotated Guide to the Constitution.* New York, NY: Stonesong Press, 2003.

Peltrason, J. W., and Sue Davis. *Understanding the Constitution.* Orlando, FL: Harcourt College Publishers, 2000.

Rakove, Jack N. *Original Meanings: Politics and Ideas in the Making of the Constitution.* New York, NY: Vintage Books, 1996.

Vile, John R. *A Companion to the United States Constitution and Its Amendments.* 4th ed. Westport, CT: Praeger Publishers, 2006.

Wright, Esmond. *Fabric of Freedom: 1763–1800.* New York, NY: Hill and Wang, 1978.

INDEX

B

Barron v. Baltimore, 41
Berghuis v. Thompkins, 7
Bill of Rights, writing and ratifying of, 9, 27–29
Blockburger v. United States, 33–35
Bolling v. Sharpe, 39
Brown v. Board of Education of Topeka, 39
Brown v. Mississippi, 37
Brown v. Ohio, 35

C

Chavez v. Martinez, 50
Chicago, Burlington and Quincy Railroad Company v. Chicago, 41

D

Dolan v. City of Tigard, 51
double jeopardy clause, 12–15, 28–29, 33–35
due process clause, 18–19, 26, 27, 28, 39

E

eminent domain, 20, 40, 46, 50–51

G

grand jury clause, 9–12, 28, 31–33, 46

H

Hawaii Housing Authority v. Midkiff, 42
Hurtado v. California, 33

I

In re Gault, 45

J

just compensation clause, 19–20, 28, 29, 40–42, 46, 51

K

Kelo v. City of New London, 46

L

Lucas v. South Carolina Coastal Council, 42

M

Madison, James, 9, 23–24, 26, 27–29
Malloy v. Hogan, 37
Mason, George, 27
McCarthy Era, 40
Miranda v. Arizona, 6, 16, 31, 37, 50
Miranda warning, 6, 7, 36, 48–50

N

New York v. Quarles, 50
North, Oliver, 39

O

O'Callahan v. Parker, 46–48

P

Penn Central Transportation Company v. City of New York, 41

S

self-incrimination clause, 6, 15–18, 27, 28, 29, 36–39
Solorio v. United States, 48
Star Chamber, 16

T

Twining v. New Jersey, 36–37

U

United States v. Halper, 13

About the Author

Corona Brezina has written more than a dozen titles for Rosen Publishing. Several of her previous books have focused on American history and the U.S. justice system, including *Johnny Tremain and the American Revolution* and *Careers in Juvenile Justice*. She lives in Chicago.

Photo Credits

Cover Mark Wilson/Getty Images; cover (inset) Chip Somodevilla/Getty Images; p. 1 (top) © www.istockphoto.com/Tom Nulens; p. 1 (bottom) © www.istockphoto.com/Lee Pettet; p. 3 © www.istockphoto.com/Nic Taylor; pp. 4–5 © Bob Daemmrich/The Image Works; pp. 8, 21, 30, 43 © www.istockphoto.com/arturbo; pp. 10–11, 19, 42 © AP Images; p. 14 Comstock/Thinkstock; p. 17 Hulton Archive/Getty Images; pp. 22–23 http://en.wikipedia.org/wiki/File:Scene_at_the_Signing_of_the_Constitution_of_the_United_States.png; p. 25 Fotosearch/Getty Images; p. 28 American Antiquarian Society, Worcester, MA/The Bridgeman Art Library; p. 32 © www.istockphoto.com/Alina555; pp. 34–35 Craig Warga/NY Daily News Archive/Getty Images; p. 38 Chris Wilkins/AFP/Getty Images; p. 44 © Larry Kolvoord/The Image Works; p. 47 Joe Raedle/Getty Images; pp. 48–49 Photodisc/Thinkstock.

Editor: Karolena Bielecki; Photo Researcher: Amy Feinberg